AF270470

MIXED MARTIAL ARTS STRATEGIES

BY SEAN SHAPIRO

SportsZone

An Imprint of Abdo Publishing
abdobooks.com

abdobooks.com

Published by Abdo Publishing, a division of ABDO, PO Box 398166, Minneapolis, Minnesota 55439. Copyright © 2024 by Abdo Consulting Group, Inc. International copyrights reserved in all countries. No part of this book may be reproduced in any form without written permission from the publisher. SportsZone™ is a trademark and logo of Abdo Publishing.

Printed in the United States of America, North Mankato, Minnesota.
102023
012024

Cover Photo: Carmen Mandato/Getty Images Sport/Getty Images
Interior Photos: Sean M. Haffey/Getty Images Sport/Getty Images, 5; Jeff Bottari/Zuffa LLC/UFC/Getty Images, 6–7, 8, 24–25; Stanley Bielecki Movie Collection/Moviepix/Getty Images, 11; Jon P. Kopaloff/Getty Images Sport/Getty Images, 13, 34–35, 42; Rey Del Rio/Getty Images Sport/Getty Images, 14, 36–37; Josh Hedges/Zuffa LLC/Getty Images Sport/Getty Images, 16–17; Josh Hedges/Zuffa LLC/UFC/Getty Images, 19, 22; Jamie Squire/Allsport/Getty Images Sport/Getty Images, 20; Holly Stein/Getty Images Sport/Getty Images, 26–27; Markus Boesch/Getty Images Sport/Getty Images, 28; Eric Jamison/AP Images, 31; John Locher/AP Images, 33; Yong Teck Lim/Getty Images Sport/Getty Images, 39; Red Line Editorial, 40; AP Images, 44–45

Editors: Charlie Beattie and Patrick Donnelly
Series Designer: Joshua Olson

Library of Congress Control Number: 2023939422

Publisher's Cataloging-in-Publication Data

Names: Shapiro, Sean, author.
Title: Mixed martial arts strategies / by Sean Shapiro
Description: Minneapolis, Minnesota: Abdo Publishing, 2024 | Series: Sports strategies | Includes online resources and index.
Identifiers: ISBN 9781098292461 (lib. bdg.) | ISBN 9798384910404 (ebook)
Subjects: LCSH: Sports teams--Juvenile literature. | Teamwork (Sports)--Juvenile literature. | Athletes--Training of--Juvenile literature. | Martial arts--Juvenile literature.
Classification: DDC 796.01--dc23

TABLE OF CONTENTS

Introduction......................................4

Chapter 1
Striking..6

Chapter 2
Wrestling...16

Chapter 3
Brazilian Jiu-Jitsu...........26

Chapter 4
Muay Thai..36

GLOSSARY 46
MORE INFORMATION 47
ONLINE RESOURCES 47
INDEX 48
ABOUT THE AUTHOR 48

INTRODUCTION

Mixed martial arts (MMA) is a complex and dynamic combat sport. Its athletes must be well versed in multiple fighting styles. With its explosive growth in popularity over the past decade, MMA has become a truly global phenomenon. It draws in athletes and fans from around the world.

Despite its raw and brutal nature, MMA is more than just a test of physical strength. It's a strategic and tactical battle. The smallest mistake can mean the difference between victory and defeat. Making the sport even more challenging is that each athlete who enters the ring has a unique fighting style. Some are former boxers who are experts in striking. Others have trained in martial arts disciplines such as jiu-jitsu and Muay Thai. They use that training to defeat their opponents by forcing them to submit to complicated holds. Some fighters have combined these styles to take brand-new strategies into the ring. This makes for a fascinating spectacle each time two fighters enter the cage.

UFC fights take place in an octagon-shaped ring.

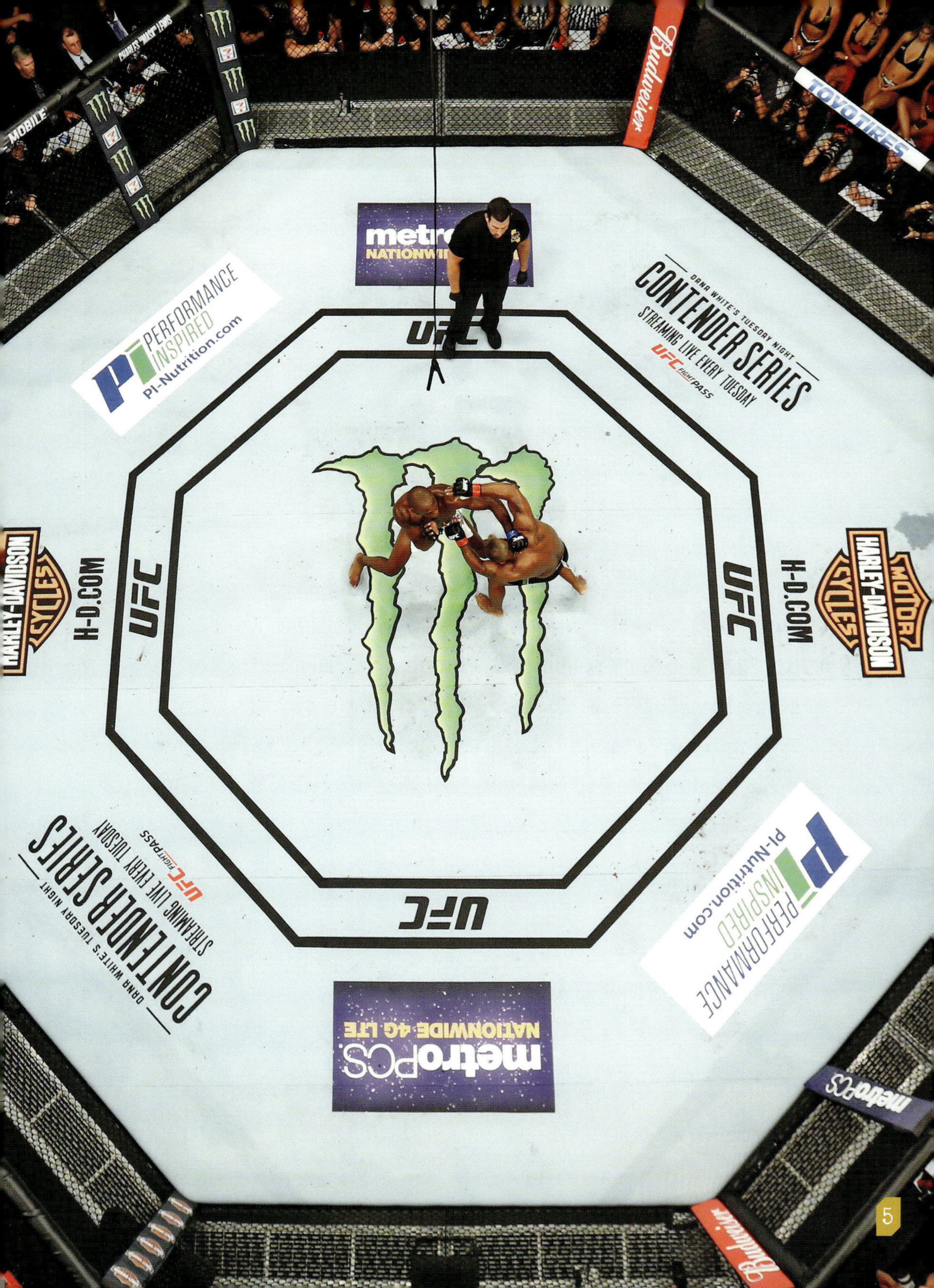

metro NATIONWIDE
PERFORMANCE INSPIRED
PI-Nutrition.com
UFC
DANA WHITE'S TUESDAY NIGHT
CONTENDER SERIES
STREAMING LIVE EVERY TUESDAY
UFC FIGHT PASS
HARLEY-DAVIDSON CYCLES
H-D.COM
UFC
UFC
H-D.COM
HARLEY-DAVIDSON MOTOR CYCLES
UFC
DANA WHITE'S TUESDAY NIGHT
CONTENDER SERIES
STREAMING LIVE EVERY TUESDAY
UFC FIGHT PASS
metroPCS NATIONWIDE 4G LTE
PERFORMANCE INSPIRED
PI-Nutrition.com
Budweiser
TOYO TIRES
MOBILE
metroPCS
Budweiser

CHAPTER 1

STRIKING

New Zealanders Israel Adesanya and Robert Whittaker faced off in the main event of Ultimate Fighting Championship (UFC) 243 on October 6, 2019, at the Marvel Stadium in Melbourne, Australia. The highly anticipated bout was held to unify the interim and undisputed UFC Middleweight Championships.

From the start, both fighters exchanged heavy blows with tremendous speed and precision. Whittaker, the reigning champion, wanted to assert his physical dominance.

Israel Adesanya enters the arena before his October 2019 fight with Robert Whittaker.

UFC
Reebok
TA
STYLE
BENDER
ISRAEL ADESANYA
UFC

Adesanya connects with a left hook.

But Adesanya, known for his elusive footwork and striking ability, refused to let that happen.

In the second round, Adesanya connected with a perfectly timed left hook that rocked Whittaker. Adesanya then followed up with a series of devastating strikes. His last blow was a powerful right hook that sent Whittaker crashing to the canvas.

The referee swiftly moved in and stopped the contest. Adesanya was the winner by knockout. With this spectacular victory, Adesanya solidified his position as one of the most dominant forces in the division. The fight was hailed as one of the most memorable middleweight title bouts in UFC history. It showcased Adesanya's exceptional striking skills and proved that he was a force to be reckoned with in the MMA world.

WHAT IS STRIKING?

Striking is one of the best-known strategies in MMA. The term refers to punching, kicking, elbowing, or kneeing an opponent. While MMA fighters mix styles, many rely on striking as their best way to win fights and potentially land knockouts.

Striking is also one of the sport's oldest strategies. It grew out of the sport of boxing. Boxing is an ancient sport. It dates to the early civilizations of Sumer and Greece. It was even part of the ancient Olympic Games. MMA likely would not exist if boxing had not become a popular sport first.

Modern boxing emerged in the 1700s. Rules governing safety were first introduced in 1867. Known as the "Marquess of Queensberry" rules, they included the use of gloves, three-minute rounds, and 10-second counts for knockdowns.

Over the next century, boxing grew into one of the most popular sports in the world. Fighters became huge celebrities. Some, such as Muhammad Ali in the 1960s and 1970s, became icons of the sports world.

At the same time, legendary martial artist and actor Bruce Lee was putting his own stamp on combat sports. Lee's revolutionary philosophies emphasized adaptability, efficiency, and an open-minded approach to fighting. He believed that traditional martial arts should not be bound by rigid styles. Instead, they should embrace the most effective techniques from many disciplines. That thinking laid the groundwork for modern MMA.

The sport began to grow in the United States during the 1980s. Many of those old boxing rules made their way into the new sport. When UFC began in the early 1990s, many of the new fighters were converted boxers. One of them, Art Jimmerson, even showed up to fight opponent Royce Gracie at UFC 1 in 1993 wearing one boxing glove.

However, fighters who were solely boxers had a built-in weakness. Standing upright, they

THE MARQUESS OF QUEENSBERRY RULES

A British sportsman named John Graham Chambers wrote the landmark 1867 boxing rules. However, the rules were named for his friend, John Sholto Douglas. An English nobleman, Douglas was the Ninth Marquess of Queensberry. Chambers thought Douglas's name and title would carry more weight. As such, the "Marquess of Queensberry" rules were born.

**Bruce Lee shows off his skills while filming his 1973 movie
Enter the Dragon.**

were vulnerable to opponents trained in other martial arts who could take them down. Fighters who came from other angles could easily beat those who were just boxing. As a result, boxers began using elbows, kicks, and knees, all of which became valuable ways of striking an opponent.

BEYOND BOXING

Bas Rutten was one of the first fighters to include kickboxing as a form of striking. He was a professional kickboxer before he went into MMA in 1993. Rutten focused on combining punches and kicks. One of Rutten's signature strikes was the liver shot. It was a powerful punch to the right side of his opponent's body, where the liver sits. He also used powerful leg kicks and knee strikes in his fights. Rutten was a terror in the ring. Many of his wins came from one-strike knockouts. His fierce striking led Rutten to a 28–4–1 career record.

Other MMA striking strategies originated with karate. Lyoto Machida was a UFC light heavyweight champion in 2009. Many of his top strikes were karate techniques, including front and side kicks.

Tae kwon do has also influenced MMA striking. Originally from Korea, tae kwon do is known for high kicks and acrobatic attempts when punching an opponent. Anderson Silva became

THE LIVER SHOT

The liver in a human body is important for blood circulation. It filters toxins out of the blood as it flows through the body. A powerful shot to the liver can stun a fighter, as both a large amount of toxins and blood are released at once. This drops a fighter's blood pressure rapidly, and the body's response is to go horizontal to fight the pressure change.

Lyoto Machida, *left*, connects with a side kick in a 2009 fight against Mauricio Rua.

a UFC champion in the 2000s. His flying knees and spinning back kicks came from his tae kwon do background.

In modern MMA, striking combines all of these different styles. Good MMA fighters need a boxer's footwork and balance. They also need the ability to surprise like a kickboxer or a karate master, as well as the flair of an exciting tae kwon do artist.

Conor McGregor, *left*, throws a spinning back kick during a fight in 2016.

ADESANYA, MCGREGOR, AND POIRIER

Since bursting onto the scene in the UFC, Adesanya's unique fighting style and exceptional striking ability have set him apart from his peers. The masterful striker came from a kickboxing background, where he had an incredible 75–4 record.

The New Zealander quickly translated his striking skills from kickboxing to MMA. While standing, Adesanya combines pinpoint accuracy with devastating power. He also has a diverse arsenal of strikes to keep opponents guessing.

From fast and precise jabs to powerful kicks and knee strikes, Adesanya's striking is both dynamic and versatile.

Adesanya also displays great artistry and showmanship. Often compared to a dancer inside the cage, Adesanya frequently shuffles and feints in all directions to keep his opponents off balance. He is then quick to taunt an opposing fighter who is having trouble keeping up. That style has made him one of the UFC's biggest stars. And many of his first 24 victories have come against top opponents such as Whittaker, Yoel Romero, and Paulo Costa. With such an impressive résumé, Adesanya is now considered one of the greatest middleweights in the history of the sport.

Adesanya's fighting style often draws comparisons to two legendary smaller fighters. Dustin Poirier and Conor McGregor have both fought in the flyweight and lightweight divisions. Each is known as an exceptional striker. All three fighters have incredible footwork. One of McGregor's signature moves is a spinning back kick. It helped him earn 19 knockouts in his first 28 fights. Poirier has earned a reputation as one of the toughest fighters in the UFC. He uses his striking ability to attack his opponents relentlessly. That determination helped Poirier defeat McGregor in two of the three fights the pair put on between 2014 and 2022.

CHAPTER 2

WRESTLING

On October 24, 2020, Russian MMA fighter Khabib Nurmagomedov entered the octagon at UFC 254 to fight American Justin Gaethje. Both fighters came into the bout as champions. Nurmagomedov had been the UFC lightweight champion since April 2018. But because of the COVID-19 pandemic, he was not able to leave Russia in 2020 to defend his title. By UFC rule, since Nurmagomedov hadn't fought in more than a year, his title was opened up to others.

Khabib Nurmagomedov, *right*, tries to take down Justin Gaethje during UFC 254.

Gaethje won it. Now Nurmagomedov was back to challenge for the championship once again.

The fight was a match of different styles. Nurmagomedov was one of the greatest wrestlers and grapplers in the sport's three-decade history. Gaethje was one of the most feared strikers in the lightweight division.

Gaethje went into the fight discussing how he needed to use leg kicks and powerful punches to limit Nurmagomedov's wrestling. That plan nearly worked, as Gaethje landed a number of shots in the first round. But late in the first round, Nurmagomedov scored his first takedown of the night. Gaethje appeared to be in deep trouble but was saved when the bell ended the round.

In the second round, Gaethje landed more kicks. But it took only a moment for Nurmagomedov to find an opening. He drove through a takedown and moved into a mount position. Nurmagomedov was now on top of Gaethje and could control Gaethje's movements with his arms and legs.

Nurmagomedov then rolled onto his back for better positioning and locked Gaethje in a triangle choke. Gaethje tried to tap the mat, or "tap out," indicating that he was giving up. But the referee didn't notice Gaethje's signal. Nurmagomedov choked his opponent into unconsciousness and the referee stepped in to end the fight.

Nurmagomedov finished his fight with Gaethje by using a triangle choke.

It was Nurmagomedov's last fight. When it was over, the world champion announced his retirement. He left an amazing legacy. Many consider him one of the best fighters pound for pound in UFC history. And his perfect 29–0 record showed how important wrestling is as a technique in MMA.

AN ANCIENT STYLE

Like boxing, wrestling dates to several ancient civilizations. There is historical evidence of wrestling in many cultures,

Wrestling remains a popular sport at the Olympic Games.

including ancient Egypt, Greece, Rome, India, and China. For many of these cultures, wrestling started as a form of training for soldiers. It later evolved into a sport of its own.

Wrestling was a major part of the ancient Greek Olympic Games. And when the modern Games returned in 1896, wrestling was included. Olympic wrestling includes two disciplines—Greco-Roman and freestyle.

Greco-Roman wrestling has limits on holds below the waist. Freestyle wrestling allows all types of holds.

Wrestling has also become a popular college sport in the United States. College wrestlers across the country compete for both individual and team titles. Individual titles are awarded in many weight classes. After graduating, many college wrestlers have become successful MMA fighters.

Wrestling has been a big part of MMA since the sport's early days in the 1980s. But early on wrestlers were sometimes at a disadvantage. At the time, MMA had few, if any, rules. And the fighting favored striking techniques over grabs or holds. Fights were held in a boxing-style ring. With no solid walls, only ropes, wrestlers could push opponents only so far. When the fights moved inside a cage, wrestlers had many places to pin their opponents. As the sport has evolved, wrestling has become one of MMA's dominant styles.

A wrestler tries to control the space of a fight inside the cage, which helps set the opponent up for takedowns. One popular technique is "ground-and-pound." To use it, the wrestler first takes down the opponent. The wrestler then uses his or her legs to hold down the other fighter. Only then does the attacker begin striking. The wrestler uses punches and elbows hoping to knock out the opponent or force the referee to call the fight.

Randy Couture, *right*, wrestles with Tim Sylvia during a fight in 2007.

COUTURE'S IMPACT

Randy Couture was a college wrestler at Oklahoma State. He went on to win Pan American titles in Greco-Roman wrestling while representing the United States. After his wrestling career ended, Couture moved to MMA. He made his debut at UFC 13 on May 30, 1997, in a four-man tournament. Couture's first opponent outweighed him by 75 pounds (34 kg), but

Couture wrestled his way to victory. He finished the fight by getting the bigger man in a rear-naked choke hold.

Couture was nearly 34 at his first UFC fight. But his MMA career lasted into his 40s. In March 2007, at age 43, he became the UFC's oldest champion by beating Tim Sylvia for the heavyweight title. The win came after Couture had already been inducted into the UFC Hall of Fame.

Couture helped inspire other wrestlers to get into MMA. Former wrestlers Matt Hughes and Dan Severn had lengthy UFC careers. Daniel Cormier and Kamaru Usman were both college wrestlers who later became UFC champions.

WRESTLING'S EVOLUTION

Wrestling in MMA has evolved to keep up with the sport and other techniques. Ground-and-pound is still a popular technique. However, many wrestlers now often use what is known as the "sprawl-and-brawl." That strategy is designed to ward off takedown attempts and keep both fighters standing. When an opponent attempts a takedown, a wrestler uses the sprawl technique to escape. Once both fighters are upright, the sprawl-and-brawl fighter then begins striking. To do this, wrestlers need to build on their skills by adding other fighting techniques.

Nurmagomedov is a perfect example of this. He grew up in Dagestan, the southernmost tip of western Russia. Wrestling is a way of life there. His father, Abdulmanap, was a wrestler in the army back when the country was known as the Soviet Union. Abdulmanap taught Khabib wrestling techniques when he was young. As Khabib grew he added to his fighting skill set by studying judo techniques. He also studied combat sambo, which is commonly used for self-defense. By the time he began his MMA career, the younger Nurmagomedov was ready for anything. Over 29 fights, Nurmagomedov controlled the octagon with his skills and stayed perfect along the way.

Nurmagomedov, *top*, uses ground-and-pound against Dustin Poirier during a fight in 2019.

MONSTER
ENERGY
UFC
UFC
UFC

CHAPTER 3

BRAZILIAN JIU-JITSU

On November 12, 1993, a fight instructor named Rorion Gracie teamed with promoter Art Davie to put together an MMA tournament in Denver, Colorado. The idea was an open showcase for all kinds of fighting styles. This was the first UFC event, later to be known as "UFC 1."

It didn't look much like the UFC bouts of today. There were no weight classes. And the tournament was set up so that fighters would compete in elimination matches. All of them happened on the same day.

Royce Gracie, *in white*, grapples with an opponent at UFC 1.

27

Royce Gracie, shown collecting his prize money at UFC 1, was one of the first two fighters inducted into the UFC Hall of Fame.

The event attracted fighters from all types of disciplines. But one stood above the rest. Royce Gracie was a 26-year-old Brazilian fighter and Rorion's younger brother. He submitted boxer Art Jimmerson quickly in his first fight. In his second fight, Gracie went up against experienced MMA fighter Ken Shamrock. In a heated contest, Gracie eventually submitted Shamrock with a rear-naked choke hold.

That put Gracie through to the final against a Dutch kickboxer named Gerard Gordeau. Gracie once again submitted his opponent. The Brazilian walked away with the tournament championship. He earned $50,000 in prize money. Gracie defended his title at UFC 2 and won again at UFC 4.

To those in the MMA world, Gracie was no surprise. He came from the first family of a distinct fighting tradition. Gracie's father and uncles had invented Brazilian jiu-jitsu. And at UFC 1, Gracie showed off the style to the world.

FAMILY STYLE

Brazilian jiu-jitsu is a technique that focuses on ground grappling. As Gracie demonstrated, its path to victory is through submission techniques such as locking an opponent's joints or gaining choke holds. Unlike some other techniques used in MMA, Brazilian jiu-jitsu is a fairly new style.

Royce Gracie's father was Helio Gracie. Along with his four brothers, Helio began studying Japanese jiu-jitsu in the 1920s. The Japanese version is a method of combat created in the 1500s. It was used mostly for personal defense, often to take a weapon away from an attacker. While the Japanese version was more upright, the Gracie brothers focused on ground combat. That's how Brazilian jiu-jitsu was born.

The style is less about strength than it is about leverage. Brazilian jiu-jitsu fighters try to control their opponent's movement first. Then they try to apply joint locks and chokes.

The Gracies developed their technique over the next several decades, and Brazilian jiu-jitsu became an international sport.

Royce Gracie's victories in the early UFC events sparked interest from other fighters in Brazilian jiu-jitsu. Boxers and wrestlers who were defeated by Brazilian jiu-jitsu artists wanted to learn more about the craft. They studied it themselves to become more well-rounded fighters. In 1994 the International Brazilian Jiu-Jitsu Federation was founded to oversee competitions and promote the sport globally. Despite that, many Brazilian jiu-jitsu fighters choose to fight in the UFC.

BEYOND THE GRACIES

Demian Maia made his UFC debut in 2007. Using grappling and traditional Brazilian jiu-jitsu techniques, he won his first five fights in the organization. Before long he gained a reputation as one of the best technical fighters in the sport. Known as one

Demian Maia, *left*, works to secure an armbar in a 2008 fight.

of the sport's most effective fighters at winning by submission, he showed off his submission skills well into his 40s.

Antonio Rodrigo Nogueira, better known as "Minotauro," proved Brazilian jiu-jitsu could work extremely well in the heavyweight division. He made his MMA debut in 1999 and joined the UFC in 2007. His popularity rose as he became known for his toughness and submission skills. In 2008 he was all set for a UFC heavyweight championship title shot against reigning champion Randy Couture. But Couture turned down the fight. That opened up Couture's title, so Nogueira instead fought Tim Sylvia for what is called an "interim" championship.

In the fight's third round, Nogueira caught Sylvia in what is known as a guillotine choke. After taking Sylvia's legs out and knocking him to the ground, Nogueira positioned himself on his back. He then wrapped both of his arms around Sylvia's neck and trapped his head. Nogueira also used his legs to lock up Sylvia's hips. After a few seconds of pressure on his neck, Sylvia tapped out.

Brian Ortega was just 13 when he started training with Rener Gracie, Rorion's son, in Brazilian jiu-jitsu. Six years later, in 2010, he made his MMA debut. Ortega won his first fight using a triangle choke, another Brazilian jiu-jitsu move. The triangle choke uses both legs and one arm to form a triangle around an opponent's neck.

Ortega made his UFC debut in 2014. Of his first 15 wins, seven came from submissions using Brazilian jiu-jitsu techniques. Along the way Ortega has picked up the nickname "T-City" for his mastery of the triangle choke.

A NECESSARY TOOL

Brazilian jiu-jitsu has evolved a great deal since Royce Gracie's win at UFC 1. In the 1990s, it was not well-known in the wider fighting world. Now Brazilian jiu-jitsu is a necessary training

Brian Ortega, *bottom*, puts his opponent in a triangle choke during UFC 195.

tool for every mixed martial artist. Most successful fighters use elements of the technique in their fighting styles in modern MMA. Nearly all MMA gyms offer individual Brazilian jiu-jitsu classes.

Canadian Georges St.-Pierre is considered one of the best UFC fighters of all time. St.-Pierre was a great striker. But he added Brazilian jiu-jitsu to his skill set to make him a complete fighter.

St.-Pierre was known for his use of the guard position. Brazilian jiu-jitsu fighters use that position to control their opponent's body by using their own as a shield. From there, fighters can use their legs to lock up an opponent. One of St.-Pierre's main weapons was the butterfly guard. While on his back, he positioned his shins inside an opponent's hips to control their legs. From there, he could sweep the other fighter into position to gain a submission. St.-Pierre retired in 2019 having won 26 of his 28 career fights, with six victories coming by submission. He won both the welterweight and middleweight titles during his UFC career.

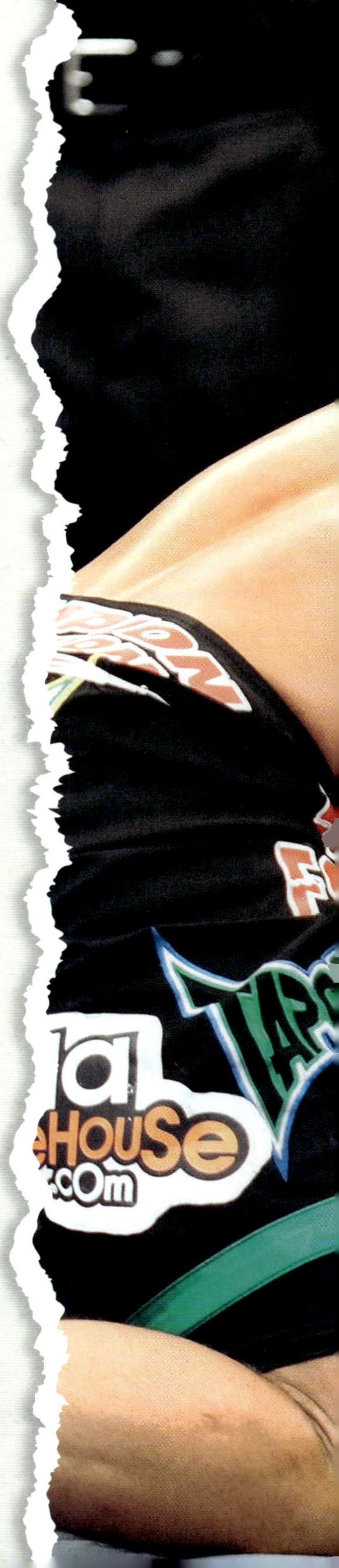

Georges St.-Pierre, *bottom*, grapples in the guard position against Thiago Alves at UFC 100.

CHAPTER 4

MUAY THAI

On June 8, 2019, Kyrgyzstani fighter Valentina Shevchenko defended her UFC women's flyweight championship in dominant fashion against American Jessica Eye. Shevchenko set the tone in the first round, loading up some big kicks with her left leg that pushed Eye back. Eventually Shevchenko pinned Eye against the cage of the octagon. Instead of keeping her there, Shevchenko allowed Eye back into the center of the ring. That way Shevchenko could reload for more attacks.

Valentina Shevchenko, *left*, is known for her vicious kicks.

Eye withstood the first round barrage. The fighters maneuvered around the ring early in the second. Then, 26 seconds into the round, Eye opened up to try to throw a punch. Shevchenko whipped her left leg around with lightning speed. The kick caught Eye squarely in the side of the head. She crashed to the canvas. It was instantly clear that Eye was unconscious. The fight was over.

Shevchenko is widely regarded as one of the best female fighters in the world. Her striking skills were honed through years of Muay Thai training. They are a significant part of her success in MMA.

Shevchenko's Muay Thai background is evident in her striking style, which is characterized by her technical precision and devastating power. She is known for her ability to land strikes from a variety of angles and ranges, and her kicks, knees, and elbows are particularly devastating.

In MMA Shevchenko has used her Muay Thai skills to great effect,

THE FAMILY BUSINESS

Valentina Shevchenko began training at a young age under the guidance of her mother, Elena, who was a Muay Thai instructor. Elena was the president of Kyrgyzstan's national Muay Thai association before the family moved to Peru.

Shevchenko, *right*, is comfortable keeping her distance or striking from close range.

dominating opponents with her striking and finishing fights with brutal knockouts. She is also highly effective in the clinch, where her Muay Thai background allows her to control opponents and land strikes with precision.

MUAY THAI HISTORY

Like many forms of martial arts, Muay Thai began as a military training exercise. Its history dates back to the 1500s in present-day Thailand. There, the style was created to help soldiers in combat.

At that time, soldiers were often engaged in battles both on foot and on horseback. They needed a close-range fighting style they could use to both defend themselves and attack

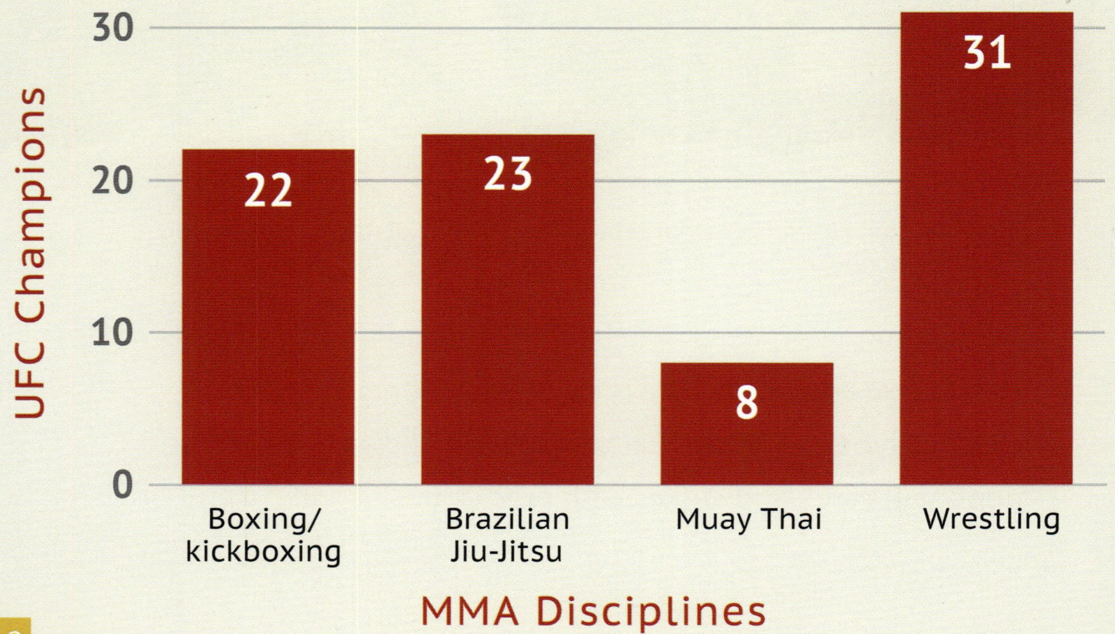

their enemies. Muay Thai was born out of that need. It quickly became an important part of the culture. Over the centuries, Muay Thai evolved into a popular sport. Fighters competed in tournaments and matches throughout Thailand. The sport became so popular that it was eventually recognized as the country's national sport.

Muay Thai was initially known as *"Muay Boran,"* which means "ancient boxing." However, it evolved into its modern form during the 20th century and came to be known as Muay Thai, taking its name from the country where it was invented. In the mid-20th century, Muay Thai became increasingly popular outside of Thailand. Fighters from other countries often traveled to the Asian nation to learn and compete in the sport.

Muay Thai is known for its striking techniques. The style emphasizes powerful strikes and quick footwork. It is also known for its intense training regimens and conditioning routines. Muay Thai fighters typically train for several hours each day. They focus on developing their strength, speed, and endurance.

"CRO COP" REVOLUTION

In the late 1990s and early 2000s, Muay Thai fighters such as Maurice Smith and Mirko "Cro Cop" Filipović began to make

Mirko "Cro Cop" Filipović prepares to deliver a head kick during a fight in 2009.

waves in MMA. They showcased their devastating striking skills and knocked out opponents with powerful kicks and knees. Cro Cop in particular helped grow both MMA and Muay Thai's popularity. The "Cro Cop Kick" is a left-footed head kick, similar to the one that Shevchenko delivered to Eye. It pops up on many MMA highlight reels.

Cro Cop was a professional kickboxer before transitioning to MMA. His Muay Thai skills made that switch possible. Cro Cop was known for his brutal elbow strikes, another technique that is commonly used in Muay Thai. But he was also excellent at clinching. This was another lesson taken from Muay Thai.

The discipline was developed specifically for fighting in close quarters. Cro Cop was able to control his opponents and deliver knees and other strikes while in the clinch.

Cro Cop helped Muay Thai become a staple of MMA. Later fighters such as Anderson Silva, Joanna Jędrzejczyk, and Shevchenko followed in his path. Silva is considered one of the greatest fighters of all time.

AN EXCITING STYLE

Silva started his career in Muay Thai, training and competing in the sport in his native Brazil. He is known for his fluid and unpredictable striking style. It incorporates elements of several martial arts, but mainly Muay Thai and boxing.

Silva's Muay Thai skills are particularly evident in his use of knee strikes and kicks. He has been known to use various Muay Thai kicks, such as the teep (which is also known as a push kick), the roundhouse kick, and the high kick in his fights. One of his most famous knockouts came against Rich Franklin in 2006. Early in the first round, Silva executed a Muay Thai clinch in which he clamped his hands around the back of Franklin's head and used his elbows to keep Franklin's arms outside. Silva then unleashed a series of close-range knees to Franklin's ribs. When Franklin moved his arms down to cover his body, Silva aimed his knee at Franklin's head. After delivering that

punishment for more than a minute, Silva knocked Franklin to the canvas. The referee moved in and stopped the fight.

The knockout is one of the most exciting elements for fans of any combat sport. And that makes Muay Thai a crowd-pleasing strategy. With its combination of lightning-fast foot, knee, and fist strikes, the style lends itself to ending fights in a split second. Of Silva's first 34 MMA wins, 23 came by knockout. Shevchenko's win over Eye was no fluke either. Shevchenko racked up eight knockouts in her first 23 victories.

That type of excitement is exactly why MMA has become so popular. The fights are intense. The fighters are athletic and strong. And a match can end at any moment with a well-placed strike. That combination of action and drama keeps fans coming back for more.

Anderson Silva, *right*, throws a push kick in a fight in 2010.

GLOSSARY

cage
The fighting space used in MMA that includes a fence surrounding a mat. In the UFC, the cage is in the shape of an octagon.

civilizations
Cultures that existed for various periods of time throughout human history.

clinch
A hold between two fighters who are close to each other.

evolved
Changed over time.

grappling
Hand-to-hand combat with the goal of gaining control over and submitting an opponent.

icons
People who are well known for excellence in a certain field.

knockout
A strike that knocks an opponent down and leaves them unable to get up again.

pound for pound
A term used to compare the abilities of fighters from different weight classes.

promoter
Someone who puts together and advertises events for spectators.

submit
Force an opponent to quit a fight by tapping out.

BOOKS

Krohn, Frazer Andrew. *MMA: Female Fighters*. Minneapolis, MN: Abdo Publishing, 2023.

Krohn, Frazer Andrew. *MMA: Ferocious Fighting Styles*. Minneapolis, MN: Abdo Publishing, 2023.

Krohn, Frazer Andrew. *MMA: Lasting Legends*. Minneapolis, MN: Abdo Publishing, 2023.

ONLINE RESOURCES

To learn more about mixed martial arts strategies, please visit **abdobooklinks.com** or scan this QR code. These links are routinely monitored and updated to provide the most current information available.

INDEX

Adesanya, Israel, 6–9, 14–15
Ali, Muhammad, 9

Chambers, John Graham, 10
Cormier, Daniel, 23
Costa, Paulo, 15
Couture, Randy, 22–23, 31–32

Dagestan, Russia, 24
Davie, Art, 26
Denver, Colorado, 26
Douglas, John Sholto, 10

Eye, Jessica, 36–38, 42, 45

Filipović, Mirko, 41–43
Franklin, Mitch, 43–45

Gaethje, Justin, 16–18
Gordeau, Gerard, 28, 30
Gracie, Helio, 29, 30
Gracie, Rener, 32
Gracie, Rorion, 26, 30, 32
Gracie, Royce, 10, 28–30, 32

Hughes, Matt, 23

Jędrzejczyk, Joanna, 43
Jimmerson, Art, 10, 28, 30

Lee, Bruce, 10

Machida, Lyoto, 12
Maia, Demian, 30–31
McGregor, Conor, 15
Melbourne, Australia, 6

Nogueira, Rodrigo (Minotauro), 31–32
Nurmagomedov, Abdulmanap, 24
Nurmagomedov, Khabib, 16–19, 24

Ortega, Brian, 32

Poirier, Dustin, 15

Romero, Yoel, 15
Rutten, Bas, 12

Severn, Dan, 23
Shamrock, Ken, 28, 30
Shevchenko, Elena, 38
Shevchenko, Valentina, 36–39, 42–45
Silva, Anderson, 12–13, 43–45
Smith, Maurice, 41–42
St.-Pierre, Georges, 33–34
Sylvia, Tim, 23, 32

Usman, Kamaru, 23

Whittaker, Robert, 6–8, 15

ABOUT THE AUTHOR

Sean Shapiro is a freelance author and journalist living in Michigan. He and his wife, Christina, are the proud parents of Evangeline and Dean.